The Kosher Konundrum: A Culinary Guide to Greek Jewish Cuisine

Unraveling the Culinary Secrets of the Sephardic Diaspora

Introduction

Welcome to the Kosher Konundrum, a culinary journey through the vibrant and enigmatic world of Greek Jewish cuisine. This cookbook is your guide to unlocking the secrets of the Sephardic diaspora, where the flavors of the Mediterranean meet the traditions of Judaism.

For centuries, Jews have thrived in Greece, their culture and cuisine intertwining with the local heritage. The result is a unique culinary tapestry that reflects the rich history and vibrant spirit of this ancient land.

This cookbook is more than just a collection of recipes; it is a celebration of the Jewish experience in Greece. Through these pages, you will discover the culinary advantages that Greek Jews have enjoyed, including access to fresh Mediterranean ingredients, a strong tradition of home cooking, and a deep understanding of Jewish dietary laws.

Advantages of Greek Jewish Cuisine

- ***Fresh, Mediterranean ingredients:*** Greece is a culinary paradise, with an abundance of fresh fruits, vegetables, herbs, and seafood. Greek Jews have long taken advantage of these ingredients to create delicious and healthy dishes.

- ***Strong tradition of home cooking:*** Family meals are an important part of Jewish culture, and Greek Jews are no exception. Many of the recipes in this cookbook have been passed down through generations, ensuring that traditional flavors and techniques are preserved.

- ***Deep understanding of Jewish dietary laws:*** Greek Jews have a deep understanding of kashrut, the Jewish dietary laws. This ensures that all of the recipes in this cookbook are kosher, so you can enjoy them with confidence.

Tips and Cooking Techniques

- ***Use high-quality ingredients:*** The best Greek Jewish dishes start with the best ingredients. Use fresh, seasonal produce and high-quality meat and fish.

- ***Don't be afraid to experiment:*** Greek Jewish cuisine is a fusion of flavors, so feel free to experiment with different ingredients and techniques.

- ***Cook with love:*** The most important ingredient in any dish is love. Cook with care and attention, and your food will be all the more delicious.

Main Ingredients

- ***Olive oil:*** Olive oil is a staple of Greek cuisine, and it is used extensively in Greek Jewish cooking. It adds flavor, richness, and الصحية to dishes.

- ***Lemon:*** Lemons are another important ingredient in Greek Jewish cuisine. They add a bright, citrusy flavor to dishes.

- ***Garlic:*** Garlic is a key ingredient in many Greek Jewish dishes. It adds a savory, aromatic flavor.

- ***Herbs:*** Herbs are used extensively in Greek Jewish cooking. Common herbs include oregano, thyme, rosemary, and basil.

Other Useful Information

- ***Kosher glossary:*** This cookbook includes a glossary of kosher terms to help you understand the dietary laws.

- ***Conversion charts:*** This cookbook includes conversion charts to help you convert measurements between different units.

- ***Index:*** This cookbook includes an index to help you find recipes easily.

We hope you enjoy this culinary journey through the Kosher Konundrum. May your meals be filled with flavor, tradition, and joy!

Breakfast

1. Shakshuka with Feta and Olives

Ingredients:

- 1 tablespoon olive oil
- 1 onion, chopped
- 2 cloves garlic, minced
- 1 red bell pepper, chopped
- 1 green bell pepper, chopped
- 2 (15 ounce) cans diced tomatoes
- 1 teaspoon ground cumin
- 1 teaspoon ground coriander
- 1/2 teaspoon paprika
- 1/4 teaspoon cayenne pepper
- 1/2 teaspoon salt
- 1/4 teaspoon black pepper
- 6 eggs
- 1/2 cup crumbled feta cheese
- 1/4 cup chopped olives

Approximate Nutritional Values:

- Calories: 300
- Fat: 15 grams
- Protein: 20 grams
- Carbohydrates: 25 grams

Complete Detailed Preparation:

1. Heat the olive oil in a large skillet over medium heat.
2. Add the onion and cook until softened, about 5 minutes.
3. Add the garlic and cook for 1 minute more.
4. Add the bell peppers and cook until softened, about 5 minutes.
5. Stir in the diced tomatoes, cumin, coriander, paprika, cayenne pepper, salt, and black pepper.
6. Bring to a simmer and cook for 15 minutes, or until the sauce has thickened.
7. Crack the eggs into the skillet and carefully space them out.
8. Cover and cook until the eggs are cooked to your desired doneness, about 5 minutes for runny eggs or 10 minutes for hard-cooked eggs.
9. Sprinkle the feta cheese and olives over the eggs.
10. Serve immediately with pita bread or toast.

Variants:

- Add other vegetables to the shakshuka, such as zucchini, mushrooms, or spinach.
- Use different types of cheese, such as goat cheese or mozzarella cheese.
- Add a dollop of Greek yogurt or sour cream to the top of the shakshuka.

Tips:

- For a spicier shakshuka, add more cayenne pepper.
- If you don't have a skillet, you can make shakshuka in a baking dish.

- Shakshuka can be served for breakfast, lunch, or dinner.

Notes:

- This recipe is for a basic shakshuka. You can add other ingredients to your liking, such as chorizo, sausage, or beans.
- Shakshuka is a great way to use up leftover vegetables.
- Shakshuka can be made ahead of time and reheated when you're ready to serve.

2. Spinach and Feta Borekas

Ingredients:

- 1 package (1 pound) frozen spinach, thawed and squeezed dry
- 1 cup crumbled feta cheese
- 1/2 cup chopped onion
- 1/4 cup chopped fresh dill
- 1/4 cup olive oil
- 1 teaspoon salt
- 1/2 teaspoon black pepper
- 1 package (1 pound) phyllo dough, thawed
- 1/2 cup melted butter

Approximate Nutritional Values:

- Calories: 250
- Fat: 15 grams
- Protein: 10 grams
- Carbohydrates: 25 grams

Complete Detailed Preparation:

1. Preheat oven to 375 degrees F (190 degrees C).
2. In a large bowl, combine the spinach, feta cheese, onion, dill, olive oil, salt, and black pepper.
3. Unroll the phyllo dough and cut it into 12 equal squares.
4. Place a spoonful of the spinach mixture in the center of each square.
5. Fold the corners of the phyllo dough over the filling to form a triangle.
6. Brush the borekas with melted butter.
7. Place the borekas on a baking sheet and bake for 20-25 minutes, or until golden brown.
8. Serve warm.

Variants:

- Add other vegetables to the filling, such as chopped zucchini, mushrooms, or peppers.
- Use different types of cheese, such as goat cheese or mozzarella cheese.
- Add a dollop of Greek yogurt or sour cream to the filling.

Tips:

- To make the borekas ahead of time, bake them according to the directions and then let them cool completely. Store the borekas in an airtight container in the refrigerator for up to 3 days. When you're ready to serve, reheat the borekas in a preheated oven at 350 degrees F (175 degrees C) for 10-15 minutes, or until warmed through.
- If you don't have phyllo dough, you can use puff pastry instead.

Notes:

- Borekas are a popular Greek appetizer or snack. They are often served with a dipping sauce, such as tzatziki or hummus.
- Borekas can be made in a variety of shapes and sizes. The most common shape is the triangle, but you can also make them into squares, rectangles, or even circles.

3. Greek Yogurt with Honey and Walnuts

Ingredients:

- 1 cup Greek yogurt
- 1 tablespoon honey
- 1/4 cup chopped walnuts

Approximate Nutritional Values:

- Calories: 200
- Fat: 10 grams
- Protein: 20 grams
- Carbohydrates: 20 grams

Complete Detailed Preparation:

1. In a small bowl, combine the Greek yogurt, honey, and walnuts.
2. Stir until well combined.
3. Serve immediately.

Variants:

- Add other toppings to your Greek yogurt, such as fruit, granola, or chocolate chips.
- Use different types of nuts, such as almonds, pistachios, or pecans.
- Drizzle your Greek yogurt with a little bit of olive oil for extra flavor.

Tips:

- For a thicker yogurt, strain it overnight in the refrigerator.
- If you don't have honey, you can use maple syrup or agave nectar instead.
- Greek yogurt is a great source of protein and calcium.

Notes:

- Greek yogurt with honey and walnuts is a popular breakfast or snack in Greece.
- It is a simple and delicious way to enjoy the health benefits of Greek yogurt.
- Greek yogurt can be used in a variety of recipes, both sweet and savory.

4. Scrambled Eggs with Tomatoes and Herbs

Ingredients:

- 2 tablespoons olive oil
- 1/2 onion, chopped
- 1 clove garlic, minced
- 1 cup chopped tomatoes
- 1/4 cup chopped fresh herbs, such as basil, oregano, or thyme
- 6 eggs
- 1/4 cup grated Parmesan cheese
- Salt and pepper to taste

Approximate Nutritional Values:

- Calories: 250
- Fat: 15 grams
- Protein: 20 grams
- Carbohydrates: 10 grams

Complete Detailed Preparation:

1. Heat the olive oil in a large skillet over medium heat.
2. Add the onion and cook until softened, about 5 minutes.
3. Add the garlic and cook for 1 minute more.
4. Add the tomatoes and herbs and cook until the tomatoes have softened, about 5 minutes.
5. In a bowl, whisk together the eggs, Parmesan cheese, salt, and pepper.
6. Pour the egg mixture into the skillet and cook, stirring constantly, until the eggs are cooked to your desired doneness.
7. Serve immediately.

Variants:

- Add other vegetables to the scrambled eggs, such as chopped peppers, mushrooms, or spinach.
- Use different types of cheese, such as feta cheese or goat cheese.
- Add a dollop of Greek yogurt or sour cream to the scrambled eggs.

Tips:

- For fluffier scrambled eggs, whisk the eggs vigorously before cooking.
- Cook the scrambled eggs over medium heat to prevent them from burning.
- Don't overcook the scrambled eggs, or they will become tough.

Notes:

- Scrambled eggs with tomatoes and herbs is a popular breakfast dish in Greece.
- It is a simple and delicious way to enjoy the flavors of the Mediterranean.
- Scrambled eggs can be served with a variety of sides, such as toast, pita bread, or fruit.

5. Bourekas Tiropita (Cheese Pie)

Ingredients:

For the dough:

- 2 cups all-purpose flour
- 1 teaspoon salt
- 1/2 cup olive oil
- 1/2 cup water

For the filling:

- 1 pound feta cheese, crumbled
- 1/2 cup grated Parmesan cheese
- 1/4 cup chopped fresh parsley
- 1/4 cup chopped fresh dill
- 1/4 cup olive oil
- 1 egg, beaten

Approximate Nutritional Values:

- Calories: 300
- Fat: 20 grams
- Protein: 15 grams
- Carbohydrates: 25 grams

Complete Detailed Preparation:

For the dough:

1. In a large bowl, combine the flour and salt.
2. Add the olive oil and water and mix until a dough forms.
3. Knead the dough for 5-7 minutes until it is smooth and elastic.
4. Wrap the dough in plastic wrap and let it rest for at least 30 minutes.

For the filling:

1. In a large bowl, combine the feta cheese, Parmesan cheese, parsley, dill, olive oil, and egg.
2. Mix well until all of the ingredients are combined.

To assemble the bourekas:

1. Preheat the oven to 375 degrees F (190 degrees C).
2. Divide the dough into 12 equal pieces.
3. Roll out each piece of dough into a thin circle.
4. Place a spoonful of the filling in the center of each circle.
5. Fold the dough over the filling to form a triangle.
6. Crimp the edges of the dough to seal.
7. Place the bourekas on a baking sheet and brush with olive oil.
8. Bake for 20-25 minutes, or until golden brown.
9. Serve warm.

Variants:

- Add other ingredients to the filling, such as chopped spinach, mushrooms, or onions.
- Use different types of cheese, such as goat cheese or mozzarella cheese.

- Add a dollop of Greek yogurt or sour cream to the filling.

Tips:

- To make the bourekas ahead of time, bake them according to the directions and then let them cool completely. Store the bourekas in an airtight container in the refrigerator for up to 3 days. When you're ready to serve, reheat the bourekas in a preheated oven at 350 degrees F (175 degrees C) for 10-15 minutes, or until warmed through.
- If you don't have time to make your own dough, you can use store-bought puff pastry instead.

Notes:

- Bourekas tiropita is a popular Greek appetizer or snack.
- It is a simple and delicious way to enjoy the flavors of Greece.
- Bourekas can be served with a variety of dipping sauces, such as tzatziki or hummus.

6. Spanakopita (Spinach Pie)

Ingredients:

For the dough:

- 2 cups all-purpose flour
- 1 teaspoon salt
- 1/2 cup olive oil
- 1/2 cup water

For the filling:

- 1 pound spinach, washed and chopped
- 1/2 onion, chopped
- 1 clove garlic, minced
- 1/4 cup chopped fresh parsley
- 1/4 cup chopped fresh dill
- 1/4 cup olive oil
- 1/2 cup feta cheese, crumbled
- 1/2 cup ricotta cheese
- 1 egg, beaten
- Salt and pepper to taste

Approximate Nutritional Values:

- Calories: 350
- Fat: 25 grams
- Protein: 15 grams
- Carbohydrates: 30 grams

Complete Detailed Preparation:

For the dough:

1. In a large bowl, combine the flour and salt.
2. Add the olive oil and water and mix until a dough forms.
3. Knead the dough for 5-7 minutes until it is smooth and elastic.
4. Wrap the dough in plastic wrap and let it rest for at least 30 minutes.

For the filling:

1. In a large skillet, heat the olive oil over medium heat.
2. Add the onion and cook until softened, about 5 minutes.
3. Add the garlic and cook for 1 minute more.
4. Add the spinach, parsley, and dill and cook until the spinach is wilted, about 5 minutes.
5. In a large bowl, combine the spinach mixture, feta cheese, ricotta cheese, egg, salt, and pepper.
6. Mix well until all of the ingredients are combined.

To assemble the spanakopita:

1. Preheat the oven to 375 degrees F (190 degrees C).
2. Divide the dough into 12 equal pieces.
3. Roll out each piece of dough into a thin circle.
4. Place a spoonful of the filling in the center of each circle.

5. Fold the dough over the filling to form a triangle.
6. Crimp the edges of the dough to seal.
7. Place the spanakopita on a baking sheet and brush with olive oil.
8. Bake for 20-25 minutes, or until golden brown.
9. Serve warm.

Variants:

- Add other ingredients to the filling, such as chopped mushrooms, zucchini, or leeks.
- Use different types of cheese, such as goat cheese or mozzarella cheese.
- Add a dollop of Greek yogurt or sour cream to the filling.

Tips:

- To make the spanakopita ahead of time, bake it according to the directions and then let it cool completely. Store the spanakopita in an airtight container in the refrigerator for up to 3 days. When you're ready to serve, reheat the spanakopita in a preheated oven at 350 degrees F (175 degrees C) for 10-15 minutes, or until warmed through.
- If you don't have time to make your own dough, you can use store-bought puff pastry instead.

Notes:

- Spanakopita is a popular Greek appetizer or snack.
- It is a simple and delicious way to enjoy the flavors of Greece.
- Spanakopita can be served with a variety of dipping sauces, such as tzatziki or hummus.

7. Tyropita (Cheese Pie)

Ingredients:

For the dough:

- 2 cups all-purpose flour
- 1 teaspoon salt
- 1/2 cup olive oil
- 1/2 cup water

For the filling:

- 1 pound feta cheese, crumbled
- 1/2 cup grated Parmesan cheese
- 1/4 cup chopped fresh parsley
- 1/4 cup chopped fresh dill
- 1/4 cup olive oil
- 1 egg, beaten
- Salt and pepper to taste

Approximate Nutritional Values:

- Calories: 300
- Fat: 20 grams
- Protein: 15 grams
- Carbohydrates: 25 grams

Complete Detailed Preparation:

For the dough:

1. In a large bowl, combine the flour and salt.
2. Add the olive oil and water and mix until a dough forms.
3. Knead the dough for 5-7 minutes until it is smooth and elastic.
4. Wrap the dough in plastic wrap and let it rest for at least 30 minutes.

For the filling:

1. In a large bowl, combine the feta cheese, Parmesan cheese, parsley, dill, olive oil, egg, salt, and pepper.
2. Mix well until all of the ingredients are combined.

To assemble the tyropita:

1. Preheat the oven to 375 degrees F (190 degrees C).
2. Divide the dough into 12 equal pieces.
3. Roll out each piece of dough into a thin circle.
4. Place a spoonful of the filling in the center of each circle.
5. Fold the dough over the filling to form a triangle.
6. Crimp the edges of the dough to seal.
7. Place the tyropita on a baking sheet and brush with olive oil.
8. Bake for 20-25 minutes, or until golden brown.
9. Serve warm.

Variants:

- Add other ingredients to the filling, such as chopped spinach, mushrooms, or onions.
- Use different types of cheese, such as goat cheese or mozzarella cheese.
- Add a dollop of Greek yogurt or sour cream to the filling.

Tips:

- To make the tyropita ahead of time, bake it according to the directions and then let it cool completely. Store the tyropita in an airtight container in the refrigerator for up to 3 days. When you're ready to serve, reheat the tyropita in a preheated oven at 350 degrees F (175 degrees C) for 10-15 minutes, or until warmed through.
- If you don't have time to make your own dough, you can use store-bought puff pastry instead.

Notes:

- Tyropita is a popular Greek appetizer or snack.
- It is a simple and delicious way to enjoy the flavors of Greece.
- Tyropita can be served with a variety of dipping sauces, such as tzatziki or hummus.

8. Loukoumades (Greek Doughnuts)

Ingredients:

- 1 pound all-purpose flour
- 1 teaspoon active dry yeast
- 1/2 teaspoon sugar
- 1/2 teaspoon salt
- 1 cup warm water (110-115 degrees F)
- 1/4 cup olive oil, plus more for greasing the pan
- 1/2 cup honey
- 1/4 cup granulated sugar
- 1 teaspoon ground cinnamon

Approximate Nutritional Values:

- Calories: 250
- Fat: 10 grams
- Protein: 5 grams
- Carbohydrates: 40 grams

Complete Detailed Preparation:

1. In a large bowl, combine the flour, yeast, sugar, and salt.
2. Add the warm water and olive oil and mix until a dough forms.
3. Knead the dough for 5-7 minutes until it is smooth and elastic.
4. Place the dough in a greased bowl, cover it with plastic wrap, and let it rise in a warm place for 1 hour, or until doubled in size.
5. Punch down the dough and divide it into 12 equal pieces.
6. Roll each piece of dough into a ball and place it on a greased baking sheet.
7. Cover the baking sheet with plastic wrap and let the dough rise for another 30 minutes, or until doubled in size.
8. Heat the olive oil in a large skillet over medium heat.
9. Fry the dough balls in the hot oil for 2-3 minutes per side, or until golden brown.
10. Remove the dough balls from the oil and drain them on paper towels.
11. In a small bowl, combine the honey, granulated sugar, and cinnamon.
12. Dip the dough balls in the honey mixture and serve immediately.

Variants:

- Add other ingredients to the honey mixture, such as chopped nuts, dried fruit, or chocolate chips.
- Dust the loukoumades with powdered sugar instead of dipping them in honey.
- Fill the loukoumades with a variety of fillings, such as chocolate, custard, or fruit preserves.

Tips:

- To make the loukoumades ahead of time, fry them according to the directions and then let them cool completely. Store the loukoumades in an airtight container at room temperature for up to 2 days. When you're ready to serve, reheat the loukoumades in a preheated oven at 350 degrees F (175 degrees C) for 10-15 minutes, or until warmed through.

- If you don't have a deep fryer, you can fry the loukoumades in a large saucepan or Dutch oven.

Notes:

- Loukoumades are a popular Greek dessert.
- They are often served with honey and cinnamon, but they can also be filled with a variety of fillings.
- Loukoumades are a delicious and easy-to-make treat that is perfect for any occasion.

9. Kataifi with Nuts and Honey

Ingredients:

For the kataifi:

- 1 pound kataifi dough, thawed
- 1/2 cup melted butter
- 1/2 cup chopped walnuts
- 1/2 cup chopped almonds
- 1/2 cup chopped pistachios
- 1/4 cup ground cinnamon

For the syrup:

- 1 cup honey
- 1/2 cup sugar
- 1/2 cup water
- 1 teaspoon lemon juice

Approximate Nutritional Values:

- Calories: 350
- Fat: 20 grams
- Protein: 10 grams
- Carbohydrates: 40 grams

Complete Detailed Preparation:

For the kataifi:

1. Preheat the oven to 350 degrees F (175 degrees C).
2. Grease a 9x13 inch baking dish.
3. In a large bowl, combine the kataifi dough, melted butter, walnuts, almonds, pistachios, and cinnamon.
4. Mix well until the kataifi dough is evenly coated.
5. Spread the kataifi mixture into the prepared baking dish and press it down firmly.
6. Bake for 25-30 minutes, or until the kataifi is golden brown.

For the syrup:

1. In a small saucepan, combine the honey, sugar, water, and lemon juice.
2. Bring to a boil over medium heat, stirring constantly.
3. Reduce heat to low and simmer for 5 minutes, or until the syrup has thickened.

To assemble the kataifi:

1. Pour the hot syrup over the hot kataifi.
2. Let the kataifi cool completely before serving.

Variants:

- Add other nuts to the kataifi, such as pecans, hazelnuts, or macadamia nuts.
- Use different spices in the kataifi, such as nutmeg, cloves, or cardamom.
- Drizzle the kataifi with chocolate sauce or caramel sauce instead of honey syrup.

Tips:

- To make the kataifi ahead of time, assemble it according to the directions and then

refrigerate it for up to 2 days. When you're ready to serve, bring the kataifi to room temperature and then drizzle it with honey syrup.
- If you don't have a 9x13 inch baking dish, you can use a smaller dish and adjust the cooking time accordingly.

Notes:

- Kataifi with nuts and honey is a popular Greek dessert.
- It is a sweet and flaky pastry that is perfect for any occasion.
- Kataifi can be served with a variety of toppings, such as whipped cream, ice cream, or fruit.

10. Galaktoboureko (Custard Pie)

Ingredients:

For the pastry:

- 1 pound phyllo dough, thawed
- 1/2 cup melted butter

For the custard:

- 4 cups milk
- 1 cup sugar
- 1/2 cup cornstarch
- 1/4 cup all-purpose flour
- 2 eggs, beaten
- 1 teaspoon vanilla extract

For the syrup:

- 1 cup sugar
- 1/2 cup water
- 1/2 cup lemon juice

Approximate Nutritional Values:

- Calories: 300
- Fat: 20 grams
- Protein: 10 grams
- Carbohydrates: 30 grams

Complete Detailed Preparation:

For the pastry:

1. Preheat the oven to 375 degrees F (190 degrees C).
2. Grease a 9x13 inch baking dish.
3. Unroll the phyllo dough and cut it into 12 equal pieces.
4. Brush each piece of phyllo dough with melted butter.
5. Layer 6 pieces of phyllo dough in the bottom of the prepared baking dish.

For the custard:

1. In a large saucepan, combine the milk, sugar, cornstarch, and flour.
2. Cook over medium heat, stirring constantly, until the mixture has thickened.
3. Remove from heat and stir in the eggs and vanilla extract.

To assemble the galaktoboureko:

1. Pour the custard over the phyllo dough in the baking dish.
2. Top with the remaining 6 pieces of phyllo dough, brushing each piece with melted butter.
3. Bake for 30-35 minutes, or until the top of the galaktoboureko is golden brown.

For the syrup:

1. In a small saucepan, combine the sugar, water, and lemon juice.
2. Bring to a boil over medium heat, stirring constantly.
3. Reduce heat to low and simmer for 5 minutes, or until the syrup has thickened.

To serve:

1. Pour the hot syrup over the hot galaktoboureko.
2. Let the galaktoboureko cool completely before serving.

Variants:

- Add other flavors to the custard, such as orange zest, cinnamon, or nutmeg.
- Use a different type of pastry, such as puff pastry or shortcrust pastry.
- Top the galaktoboureko with chopped nuts or fruit before baking.

Tips:

- To make the galaktoboureko ahead of time, assemble it according to the directions and then refrigerate it for up to 2 days. When you're ready to serve, bake the galaktoboureko according to the directions.
- If you don't have a 9x13 inch baking dish, you can use a smaller dish and adjust the cooking time accordingly.

Notes:

- Galaktoboureko is a popular Greek dessert.
- It is a rich and creamy custard pie that is perfect for any occasion.
- Galaktoboureko can be served with a variety of toppings, such as whipped cream, ice cream, or fruit.

11. Baklava

Ingredients:

For the pastry:

- 1 pound phyllo dough, thawed
- 1/2 cup melted butter

For the filling:

- 3 cups chopped walnuts
- 1 cup chopped almonds
- 1 cup chopped pistachios
- 1/2 cup sugar
- 1 teaspoon ground cinnamon
- 1/4 teaspoon ground cloves

For the syrup:

- 1 cup honey
- 1/2 cup sugar
- 1/2 cup water
- 1 tablespoon lemon juice

Approximate Nutritional Values:

- Calories: 350
- Fat: 25 grams
- Protein: 10 grams
- Carbohydrates: 30 grams

Complete Detailed Preparation:

For the pastry:

1. Preheat the oven to 350 degrees F (175 degrees C).
2. Grease a 9x13 inch baking dish.
3. Unroll the phyllo dough and cut it into 12 equal pieces.
4. Brush each piece of phyllo dough with melted butter.
5. Layer 6 pieces of phyllo dough in the bottom of the prepared baking dish.

For the filling:

1. In a large bowl, combine the walnuts, almonds, pistachios, sugar, cinnamon, and cloves.
2. Mix well.

To assemble the baklava:

1. Spread the filling evenly over the phyllo dough in the baking dish.
2. Top with the remaining 6 pieces of phyllo dough, brushing each piece with melted butter.
3. Cut the baklava into diamond shapes.

For the syrup:

1. In a small saucepan, combine the honey, sugar, water, and lemon juice.
2. Bring to a boil over medium heat, stirring constantly.
3. Reduce heat to low and simmer for 5 minutes, or until the syrup has thickened.

To serve:

1. Pour the hot syrup over the hot baklava.
2. Let the baklava cool completely before serving.

Variants:

- Add other nuts to the filling, such as hazelnuts, pecans, or macadamia nuts.
- Use different spices in the filling, such as nutmeg, cardamom, or ginger.
- Drizzle the baklava with chocolate sauce or caramel sauce instead of honey syrup.

Tips:

- To make the baklava ahead of time, assemble it according to the directions and then refrigerate it for up to 2 days. When you're ready to serve, bake the baklava according to the directions.
- If you don't have a 9x13 inch baking dish, you can use a smaller dish and adjust the cooking time accordingly.

Notes:

- Baklava is a popular Greek dessert.
- It is a rich and flaky pastry that is filled with nuts and sweetened with honey syrup.
- Baklava is a delicious and elegant dessert that is perfect for any occasion.

12. Spanakorizo (Spinach Rice)

Ingredients:

- 1 cup short-grain rice
- 2 cups water
- 1/2 onion, chopped
- 2 cloves garlic, minced
- 1 pound spinach, washed and chopped
- 1/2 cup chopped fresh dill
- 1/4 cup olive oil
- Salt and pepper to taste
- Lemon wedges, for serving

Approximate Nutritional Values:

- Calories: 250
- Fat: 10 grams
- Protein: 10 grams
- Carbohydrates: 40 grams

Complete Detailed Preparation:

1. In a medium saucepan, combine the rice, water, onion, garlic, spinach, dill, olive oil, salt, and pepper.
2. Bring to a boil over medium heat.
3. Reduce heat to low, cover, and simmer for 18 minutes, or until the rice is cooked and the liquid has been absorbed.
4. Fluff the rice with a fork and serve immediately, with lemon wedges on the side.

Variants:

- Add other vegetables to the spanakorizo, such as chopped carrots, celery, or peas.
- Use different herbs in the spanakorizo, such as oregano, basil, or thyme.
- Add a dollop of Greek yogurt or sour cream to the spanakorizo before serving.

Tips:

- To make the spanakorizo ahead of time, cook it according to the directions and then let it cool completely. Store the spanakorizo in an airtight container in the refrigerator for up to 3 days. When you're ready to serve, reheat the spanakorizo in a saucepan over medium heat, stirring occasionally.
- If you don't have short-grain rice, you can use long-grain rice instead. However, the cooking time may need to be adjusted.

Notes:

- Spanakorizo is a popular Greek dish.
- It is a simple and flavorful rice dish that is perfect for a weeknight meal.
- Spanakorizo can be served as a main course or a side dish.

13. Gigantes Plaki (Baked Giant Beans)

Ingredients:

- 1 pound dried giant beans, sorted and rinsed
- 1 onion, chopped
- 2 cloves garlic, minced
- 1 red bell pepper, chopped
- 1 green bell pepper, chopped
- 1 cup chopped tomatoes
- 1/2 cup chopped fresh parsley
- 1/4 cup olive oil
- 1 teaspoon dried oregano
- 1/2 teaspoon salt
- 1/4 teaspoon black pepper
- 1 cup vegetable broth
- 1/2 cup bread crumbs
- 1/4 cup grated Parmesan cheese

Approximate Nutritional Values:

- Calories: 300
- Fat: 15 grams
- Protein: 15 grams
- Carbohydrates: 40 grams

Complete Detailed Preparation:

1. In a large bowl, combine the beans, onion, garlic, bell peppers, tomatoes, parsley, olive oil, oregano, salt, and pepper.
2. Mix well to combine.
3. Transfer the mixture to a 9x13 inch baking dish.
4. Add the vegetable broth.
5. Cover the baking dish with foil and bake at 375 degrees F (190 degrees C) for 2 hours, or until the beans are tender.
6. In a small bowl, combine the bread crumbs and Parmesan cheese.
7. Sprinkle the bread crumb mixture over the beans.
8. Bake for an additional 15 minutes, or until the bread crumbs are golden brown.
9. Serve hot.

Variants:

- Add other vegetables to the gigantes plaki, such as chopped carrots, celery, or potatoes.
- Use different herbs in the gigantes plaki, such as basil, thyme, or rosemary.
- Add a dollop of Greek yogurt or sour cream to the gigantes plaki before serving.

Tips:

- To make the gigantes plaki ahead of time, cook it according to the directions and then let it cool completely. Store the gigantes plaki in an airtight container in the refrigerator for up to 3 days. When you're ready to serve, reheat the gigantes plaki in a preheated oven at 350 degrees F

(175 degrees C) for 15-20 minutes, or until warmed through.

- If you don't have dried giant beans, you can use canned giant beans instead. However, be sure to rinse the canned beans thoroughly before using them.

Notes:

- Gigantes plaki is a popular Greek dish.
- It is a hearty and flavorful bean dish that is perfect for a winter meal.
- Gigantes plaki can be served as a main course or a side dish.

14. Fava (Split Pea Dip)

Ingredients:

- 1 pound dried yellow split peas, sorted and rinsed
- 1 onion, chopped
- 2 cloves garlic, minced
- 1/4 cup olive oil
- 1 teaspoon dried oregano
- 1/2 teaspoon salt
- 1/4 teaspoon black pepper
- 1 cup water
- Lemon wedges, for serving

Approximate Nutritional Values:

- Calories: 200
- Fat: 10 grams
- Protein: 15 grams
- Carbohydrates: 30 grams

Complete Detailed Preparation:

1. In a large saucepan, combine the split peas, onion, garlic, olive oil, oregano, salt, pepper, and water.
2. Bring to a boil over medium heat.
3. Reduce heat to low, cover, and simmer for 1 hour, or until the split peas are tender and have broken down.
4. Remove from heat and let cool slightly.
5. Use a potato masher or immersion blender to puree the split peas until smooth.
6. Serve immediately, with lemon wedges on the side.

Variants:

- Add other vegetables to the fava, such as chopped carrots, celery, or potatoes.
- Use different herbs in the fava, such as basil, thyme, or rosemary.
- Add a dollop of Greek yogurt or sour cream to the fava before serving.

Tips:

- To make the fava ahead of time, cook it according to the directions and then let it cool completely. Store the fava in an airtight container in the refrigerator for up to 3 days. When you're ready to serve, reheat the fava in a saucepan over medium heat, stirring occasionally.
- If you don't have dried yellow split peas, you can use canned yellow split peas instead. However, be sure to rinse the canned split peas thoroughly before using them.

Notes:

- Fava is a popular Greek dip.
- It is a simple and flavorful dip that is perfect for a party or a snack.
- Fava can be served with pita bread, vegetables, or crackers.

15. Hummus

Ingredients:

- 1 can (15 ounces) chickpeas, drained and rinsed
- 1/2 cup tahini
- 1/4 cup olive oil
- 2 cloves garlic, minced
- 1/4 cup lemon juice
- 1/2 teaspoon salt
- 1/4 teaspoon black pepper
- Paprika, for garnish

Approximate Nutritional Values:

- Calories: 200
- Fat: 15 grams
- Protein: 10 grams
- Carbohydrates: 25 grams

Complete Detailed Preparation:

1. In a food processor, combine the chickpeas, tahini, olive oil, garlic, lemon juice, salt, and pepper.
2. Process until smooth and creamy.
3. Transfer the hummus to a serving bowl and garnish with paprika.
4. Serve with pita bread, vegetables, or crackers.

Variants:

- Add other ingredients to the hummus, such as chopped olives, roasted red peppers, or sun-dried tomatoes.
- Use different herbs in the hummus, such as basil, oregano, or thyme.
- Add a dollop of Greek yogurt or sour cream to the hummus before serving.

Tips:

- To make the hummus ahead of time, prepare it according to the directions and then store it in an airtight container in the refrigerator for up to 3 days. When you're ready to serve, bring the hummus to room temperature and stir it well.
- If you don't have a food processor, you can mash the chickpeas by hand. However, the hummus will not be as smooth and creamy.

Notes:

- Hummus is a popular Middle Eastern dip.
- It is a simple and flavorful dip that is perfect for a party or a snack.
- Hummus can be served with pita bread, vegetables, or crackers.

16. Tahini

Ingredients:

- 1 cup sesame seeds
- 1/4 cup olive oil

Approximate Nutritional Values:

- Calories: 150
- Fat: 15 grams
- Protein: 5 grams
- Carbohydrates: 10 grams

Complete Detailed Preparation:

1. Preheat the oven to 350 degrees F (175 degrees C).
2. Spread the sesame seeds on a baking sheet and toast in the preheated oven for 5-7 minutes, or until golden brown.
3. Remove the sesame seeds from the oven and let cool slightly.
4. In a food processor, combine the sesame seeds and olive oil.
5. Process until smooth and creamy.
6. Store the tahini in an airtight container in the refrigerator for up to 2 weeks.

Variants:

- Add other ingredients to the tahini, such as honey, maple syrup, or cocoa powder.
- Use different oils in the tahini, such as avocado oil, walnut oil, or almond oil.
- Add a dollop of tahini to smoothies, soups, or sauces for extra flavor and creaminess.

Tips:

- To make the tahini ahead of time, prepare it according to the directions and then store it in an airtight container in the refrigerator for up to 2 weeks. When you're ready to use it, bring the tahini to room temperature and stir it well.
- If you don't have a food processor, you can grind the sesame seeds in a blender or by hand using a mortar and pestle. However, the tahini will not be as smooth and creamy.

Notes:

- Tahini is a popular Middle Eastern ingredient.
- It is a versatile ingredient that can be used in a variety of dishes, including dips, sauces, and desserts.
- Tahini is a good source of healthy fats, protein, and fiber.

17. Olives

Ingredients:

- 1 pound olives
- 1 cup water
- 1/2 cup olive oil
- 1 tablespoon lemon juice
- 1 teaspoon dried oregano
- 1/2 teaspoon salt
- 1/4 teaspoon black pepper

Approximate Nutritional Values:

- Calories: 100
- Fat: 10 grams
- Protein: 2 grams
- Carbohydrates: 5 grams

Complete Detailed Preparation:

1. In a large bowl, combine the olives, water, olive oil, lemon juice, oregano, salt, and pepper.
2. Mix well to combine.
3. Cover the bowl and refrigerate for at least 2 hours, or overnight.
4. Serve the olives as an appetizer or snack.

Variants:

- Add other ingredients to the olives, such as chopped garlic, red onion, or feta cheese.
- Use different herbs in the olives, such as basil, thyme, or rosemary.
- Add a dollop of Greek yogurt or sour cream to the olives before serving.

Tips:

- To make the olives ahead of time, prepare them according to the directions and then store them in an airtight container in the refrigerator for up to 2 weeks.
- If you don't have time to marinate the olives, you can simply serve them with a drizzle of olive oil and a sprinkle of salt and pepper.

Notes:

- Olives are a popular Greek appetizer.
- They are a simple and flavorful snack that is perfect for any occasion.
- Olives are a good source of healthy fats, vitamins, and minerals.

18. Pickles

Ingredients:

- 1 pound cucumbers, sliced
- 1 cup white vinegar
- 1/2 cup water
- 1/4 cup sugar
- 1 tablespoon salt
- 1 teaspoon mustard seeds
- 1 teaspoon celery seeds
- 1/2 teaspoon dill seeds

Approximate Nutritional Values:

- Calories: 20
- Fat: 0 grams
- Protein: 1 gram
- Carbohydrates: 5 grams

Complete Detailed Preparation:

1. In a large bowl, combine the cucumbers, vinegar, water, sugar, salt, mustard seeds, celery seeds, and dill seeds.
2. Mix well to combine.
3. Cover the bowl and refrigerate for at least 2 hours, or overnight.
4. Serve the pickles as an appetizer or snack.

Variants:

- Add other vegetables to the pickles, such as carrots, onions, or peppers.
- Use different herbs and spices in the pickles, such as garlic, ginger, or turmeric.
- Add a dollop of Greek yogurt or sour cream to the pickles before serving.

Tips:

- To make the pickles ahead of time, prepare them according to the directions and then store them in an airtight container in the refrigerator for up to 2 weeks.
- If you don't have time to marinate the pickles, you can simply serve them with a drizzle of vinegar and a sprinkle of salt and pepper.

Notes:

- Pickles are a popular Greek appetizer.
- They are a simple and flavorful snack that is perfect for any occasion.
- Pickles are a good source of vitamins and minerals, and they are also low in calories.

19. Cheeses

Ingredients:

- 1 gallon of whole milk
- 1/2 cup white vinegar
- 1/4 cup lemon juice
- 1 teaspoon salt

Approximate Nutritional Values:

- Calories: 100 per ounce
- Fat: 8 grams per ounce
- Protein: 7 grams per ounce
- Carbohydrates: 1 gram per ounce

Complete Detailed Preparation:

1. In a large pot, heat the milk over medium heat until it reaches 180 degrees F (82 degrees C).
2. Remove the pot from the heat and stir in the vinegar and lemon juice.
3. Let the mixture sit for 5 minutes, or until the milk has curdled.
4. Line a colander with cheesecloth and pour the curdled milk into the colander.
5. Let the curds drain for 1 hour, or until they are firm.
6. Transfer the curds to a bowl and stir in the salt.
7. Form the curds into small balls or blocks and place them on a baking sheet.
8. Refrigerate the cheeses for at least 2 hours, or overnight.

Variants:

- Add other ingredients to the cheeses, such as herbs, spices, or nuts.
- Use different types of milk to make the cheeses, such as goat's milk or sheep's milk.
- Age the cheeses for different lengths of time to create different flavors and textures.

Tips:

- To make the cheeses ahead of time, prepare them according to the directions and then store them in an airtight container in the refrigerator for up to 2 weeks.
- If you don't have cheesecloth, you can use a clean dish towel to line the colander.

Notes:

- Cheeses are a popular Greek appetizer.
- They are a simple and flavorful snack that is perfect for any occasion.
- Cheeses are a good source of protein and calcium.

20. Fruits

Ingredients:

- 1 pound of your favorite fruits, such as apples, oranges, bananas, or grapes

Approximate Nutritional Values:

- Calories: 100 per cup
- Fat: 0 grams per cup
- Protein: 1 gram per cup
- Carbohydrates: 25 grams per cup

Complete Detailed Preparation:

1. Wash the fruits thoroughly.
2. Peel and cut the fruits into bite-sized pieces, if necessary.
3. Arrange the fruits on a plate or in a bowl.
4. Serve immediately.

Variants:

- Add other ingredients to the fruits, such as nuts, seeds, or yogurt.
- Drizzle the fruits with honey or maple syrup.
- Grill or roast the fruits for a different flavor and texture.

Tips:

- To make the fruits ahead of time, prepare them according to the directions and then store them in an airtight container in the refrigerator for up to 3 days.
- If you don't have time to prepare the fruits, you can simply buy pre-cut fruits from the grocery store.

Notes:

- Fruits are a popular Greek dessert.
- They are a simple and healthy snack that is perfect for any occasion.
- Fruits are a good source of vitamins, minerals, and fiber.

Main dishes

1. Moussaka

Ingredients:

For the eggplant:

- 1 large eggplant, peeled and sliced into 1/2-inch rounds
- 1/2 cup flour
- 1/2 cup olive oil
- Salt and pepper to taste

For the meat sauce:

- 1 pound ground beef
- 1 pound ground pork
- 1 onion, chopped
- 2 cloves garlic, minced
- 1 (28 ounce) can crushed tomatoes
- 1 (15 ounce) can tomato sauce
- 1/2 cup red wine
- 1 tablespoon dried oregano
- 1 teaspoon ground cinnamon
- Salt and pepper to taste

For the béchamel sauce:

- 1/2 cup butter
- 1/2 cup all-purpose flour
- 4 cups milk
- 1/2 teaspoon nutmeg
- Salt and pepper to taste

For the topping:

- 1/2 cup grated Parmesan cheese
- 1/4 cup bread crumbs

Approximate Nutritional Values:

- Calories: 400
- Fat: 20 grams
- Protein: 25 grams
- Carbohydrates: 30 grams

Complete Detailed Preparation:

For the eggplant:

1. Preheat the oven to 375 degrees F (190 degrees C).
2. Dredge the eggplant slices in flour and then fry them in the olive oil until golden brown on both sides.
3. Season with salt and pepper.

For the meat sauce:

1. In a large skillet, brown the ground beef and pork over medium heat.
2. Add the onion and garlic and cook until softened.

3. Stir in the crushed tomatoes, tomato sauce, red wine, oregano, cinnamon, salt, and pepper.
4. Bring to a simmer and cook for 30 minutes, or until the sauce has thickened.

For the béchamel sauce:

1. In a medium saucepan, melt the butter over medium heat.
2. Whisk in the flour and cook for 1 minute.
3. Gradually whisk in the milk until smooth.
4. Bring to a simmer and cook for 5 minutes, or until the sauce has thickened.
5. Season with nutmeg, salt, and pepper.

To assemble the moussaka:

1. Spread a layer of the eggplant slices in the bottom of a 9x13 inch baking dish.
2. Top with a layer of the meat sauce.
3. Repeat the layers.
4. Pour the béchamel sauce over the top.
5. Sprinkle with Parmesan cheese and bread crumbs.
6. Bake for 30-35 minutes, or until the moussaka is heated through and the top is golden brown.

Variants:

- Add other vegetables to the moussaka, such as zucchini, potatoes, or carrots.
- Use different types of meat in the meat sauce, such as lamb or veal.
- Top the moussaka with a layer of mashed potatoes instead of béchamel sauce.

Tips:

- To make the moussaka ahead of time, assemble it according to the directions and then refrigerate it for up to 24 hours. When you're ready to bake it, bring it to room temperature and then bake it according to the directions.
- If you don't have a 9x13 inch baking dish, you can use a smaller dish and adjust the cooking time accordingly.

Notes:

- Moussaka is a popular Greek dish.
- It is a flavorful and hearty dish that is perfect for a family meal.
- Moussaka can be served with a side of salad or bread.

2. Pastitsio

Ingredients:

For the pasta:

- 1 pound pasta sheets
- 1/2 cup olive oil
- 1 onion, chopped
- 2 cloves garlic, minced
- 1 pound ground beef
- 1 pound ground pork
- 1 (28 ounce) can crushed tomatoes
- 1 (15 ounce) can tomato sauce
- 1/2 cup red wine
- 1 tablespoon dried oregano
- 1 teaspoon ground cinnamon
- Salt and pepper to taste

For the béchamel sauce:

- 1/2 cup butter
- 1/2 cup all-purpose flour
- 4 cups milk
- 1/2 teaspoon nutmeg
- Salt and pepper to taste

For the topping:

- 1/2 cup grated Parmesan cheese
- 1/4 cup bread crumbs

Approximate Nutritional Values:

- Calories: 450
- Fat: 25 grams
- Protein: 30 grams
- Carbohydrates: 35 grams

Complete Detailed Preparation:

For the pasta:

1. Preheat the oven to 375 degrees F (190 degrees C).
2. Cook the pasta sheets according to the package directions.
3. Drain the pasta and set it aside.

For the meat sauce:

1. In a large skillet, brown the ground beef and pork over medium heat.
2. Add the onion and garlic and cook until softened.
3. Stir in the crushed tomatoes, tomato sauce, red wine, oregano, cinnamon, salt, and pepper.
4. Bring to a simmer and cook for 30 minutes, or until the sauce has thickened.

For the béchamel sauce:

1. In a medium saucepan, melt the butter over medium heat.

2. Whisk in the flour and cook for 1 minute.
3. Gradually whisk in the milk until smooth.
4. Bring to a simmer and cook for 5 minutes, or until the sauce has thickened.
5. Season with nutmeg, salt, and pepper.

To assemble the pastitsio:

1. In a 9x13 inch baking dish, spread a layer of the pasta sheets.
2. Top with a layer of the meat sauce.
3. Repeat the layers.
4. Pour the béchamel sauce over the top.
5. Sprinkle with Parmesan cheese and bread crumbs.
6. Bake for 30-35 minutes, or until the pastitsio is heated through and the top is golden brown.

Variants:

- Add other vegetables to the meat sauce, such as zucchini, potatoes, or carrots.
- Use different types of meat in the meat sauce, such as lamb or veal.
- Top the pastitsio with a layer of mashed potatoes instead of béchamel sauce.

Tips:

- To make the pastitsio ahead of time, assemble it according to the directions and then refrigerate it for up to 24 hours. When you're ready to bake it, bring it to room temperature and then bake it according to the directions.
- If you don't have a 9x13 inch baking dish, you can use a smaller dish and adjust the cooking time accordingly.

Notes:

- Pastitsio is a popular Greek dish.
- It is a flavorful and hearty dish that is perfect for a family meal.
- Pastitsio can be served with a side of salad or bread.

3. Souvlaki

Ingredients:

For the souvlaki:

- 1 pound boneless, skinless chicken breasts, cut into 1-inch pieces
- 1 pound boneless, skinless pork tenderloin, cut into 1-inch pieces
- 1/2 cup olive oil
- 1/4 cup lemon juice
- 1 tablespoon dried oregano
- 1 teaspoon ground cumin
- 1/2 teaspoon salt
- 1/4 teaspoon black pepper

For the marinade:

- 1/2 cup olive oil
- 1/4 cup red wine vinegar
- 1 tablespoon dried oregano
- 1 teaspoon ground cumin
- 1/2 teaspoon salt
- 1/4 teaspoon black pepper

For the tzatziki sauce:

- 1 cup plain Greek yogurt
- 1/2 cucumber, peeled and grated
- 1 clove garlic, minced
- 1 tablespoon olive oil
- 1/4 cup chopped fresh dill
- Salt and pepper to taste

Approximate Nutritional Values:

- Calories: 350
- Fat: 20 grams
- Protein: 30 grams
- Carbohydrates: 25 grams

Complete Detailed Preparation:

For the souvlaki:

1. In a large bowl, combine the chicken, pork, olive oil, lemon juice, oregano, cumin, salt, and pepper.
2. Mix well to coat the meat.
3. Cover the bowl and refrigerate for at least 30 minutes, or up to overnight.

For the marinade:

1. In a small bowl, whisk together the olive oil, red wine vinegar, oregano, cumin, salt, and pepper.

To make the tzatziki sauce:

1. In a medium bowl, combine the yogurt, cucumber, garlic, olive oil, dill, salt, and pepper.
2. Mix well and refrigerate for at least 30 minutes, or up to overnight.

To cook the souvlaki:

1. Preheat a grill or grill pan over medium heat.
2. Thread the chicken and pork onto skewers.
3. Brush the skewers with the marinade.
4. Grill the skewers for 10-12 minutes, or until the meat is cooked through.
5. Serve the souvlaki with the tzatziki sauce.

Variants:

- Use different types of meat for the souvlaki, such as lamb, beef, or shrimp.
- Add other vegetables to the skewers, such as onions, peppers, or tomatoes.
- Serve the souvlaki with different sauces, such as hummus, tahini, or skordalia.

Tips:

- To make the souvlaki ahead of time, marinate the meat according to the directions and then refrigerate it for up to 24 hours. When you're ready to cook it, bring the meat to room temperature and then grill it according to the directions.
- If you don't have skewers, you can use toothpicks to hold the meat together.

Notes:

- Souvlaki is a popular Greek dish.
- It is a flavorful and easy-to-make dish that is perfect for a summer cookout.
- Souvlaki can be served with a variety of sides, such as rice, potatoes, or salad.

4. Gyros

Ingredients:

For the gyros meat:

- 1 pound boneless, skinless chicken breasts, thinly sliced
- 1/2 cup olive oil
- 1/4 cup lemon juice
- 1 tablespoon dried oregano
- 1 teaspoon ground cumin
- 1/2 teaspoon salt
- 1/4 teaspoon black pepper

For the tzatziki sauce:

- 1 cup plain Greek yogurt
- 1/2 cucumber, peeled and grated
- 1 clove garlic, minced
- 1 tablespoon olive oil
- 1/4 cup chopped fresh dill
- Salt and pepper to taste

For the gyros:

- 6 pita breads
- 1/2 cup chopped tomatoes
- 1/2 cup chopped onions
- 1/4 cup chopped red cabbage
- 1/4 cup chopped feta cheese

Approximate Nutritional Values:

- Calories: 400
- Fat: 25 grams
- Protein: 35 grams
- Carbohydrates: 30 grams

Complete Detailed Preparation:

For the gyros meat:

1. In a large bowl, combine the chicken, olive oil, lemon juice, oregano, cumin, salt, and pepper.
2. Mix well to coat the chicken.
3. Cover the bowl and refrigerate for at least 30 minutes, or up to overnight.

For the tzatziki sauce:

1. In a medium bowl, combine the yogurt, cucumber, garlic, olive oil, dill, salt, and pepper.
2. Mix well and refrigerate for at least 30 minutes, or up to overnight.

To cook the gyros meat:

1. Preheat a grill or grill pan over medium heat.
2. Grill the chicken for 5-7 minutes per side, or until cooked through.
3. Thinly slice the chicken.

To assemble the gyros:

1. Spread a layer of tzatziki sauce on a pita bread.
2. Top with the sliced chicken, tomatoes, onions, red cabbage, and feta cheese.
3. Roll up the pita bread and enjoy.

Variants:

- Use different types of meat for the gyros, such as lamb, beef, or pork.
- Add other vegetables to the gyros, such as lettuce, peppers, or mushrooms.
- Serve the gyros with different sauces, such as hummus, tahini, or skordalia.

Tips:

- To make the gyros ahead of time, cook the chicken according to the directions and then refrigerate it for up to 24 hours. When you're ready to assemble the gyros, bring the chicken to room temperature and then slice it.
- If you don't have a grill, you can cook the chicken in a skillet over medium heat.

Notes:

- Gyros are a popular Greek dish.
- They are a flavorful and easy-to-make dish that is perfect for a quick and easy meal.
- Gyros can be served with a variety of sides, such as rice, potatoes, or salad.

5. Spanakopita

Ingredients:

For the filling:

- 1 pound spinach, washed and chopped
- 1 onion, chopped
- 1 clove garlic, minced
- 1/2 cup chopped fresh parsley
- 1/4 cup chopped fresh dill
- 1/4 cup olive oil
- 1/2 cup feta cheese, crumbled
- 1/2 cup ricotta cheese
- 1 egg, beaten
- Salt and pepper to taste

For the pastry:

- 1 pound phyllo dough, thawed
- 1/2 cup melted butter

Approximate Nutritional Values:

- Calories: 300
- Fat: 20 grams
- Protein: 15 grams
- Carbohydrates: 25 grams

Complete Detailed Preparation:

For the filling:

1. In a large skillet, heat the olive oil over medium heat.
2. Add the onion and cook until softened.
3. Add the garlic and cook for 1 minute more.
4. Add the spinach and cook until wilted.
5. Stir in the parsley, dill, feta cheese, ricotta cheese, egg, salt, and pepper.
6. Mix well and remove from heat.

To assemble the spanakopita:

1. Preheat the oven to 375 degrees F (190 degrees C).
2. Grease a 9x13 inch baking dish.
3. Unroll the phyllo dough and cut it into 12 equal pieces.
4. Brush each piece of phyllo dough with melted butter.
5. Layer 6 pieces of phyllo dough in the bottom of the prepared baking dish.
6. Spread the spinach filling over the phyllo dough.
7. Top with the remaining 6 pieces of phyllo dough, brushing each piece with melted butter.
8. Bake for 30-35 minutes, or until golden brown.
9. Let cool slightly before serving.

Variants:

- Add other vegetables to the filling, such as chopped mushrooms, zucchini, or leeks.

- Use different types of cheese in the filling, such as goat cheese or mozzarella cheese.
- Add a dollop of Greek yogurt or sour cream to the filling.

Tips:

- To make the spanakopita ahead of time, assemble it according to the directions and then refrigerate it for up to 24 hours. When you're ready to bake it, bring it to room temperature and then bake it according to the directions.
- If you don't have a 9x13 inch baking dish, you can use a smaller dish and adjust the cooking time accordingly.

Notes:

- Spanakopita is a popular Greek dish.
- It is a flavorful and flaky pastry that is perfect for a family meal.
- Spanakopita can be served with a side of salad or soup.

6. Tiropita

Ingredients:

For the filling:

- 1 pound feta cheese, crumbled
- 1/2 cup ricotta cheese
- 1/4 cup chopped fresh parsley
- 1/4 cup chopped fresh dill
- 1/4 cup olive oil
- 1 egg, beaten
- Salt and pepper to taste

For the pastry:

- 1 pound phyllo dough, thawed
- 1/2 cup melted butter

Approximate Nutritional Values:

- Calories: 300
- Fat: 20 grams
- Protein: 15 grams
- Carbohydrates: 25 grams

Complete Detailed Preparation:

For the filling:

1. In a large bowl, combine the feta cheese, ricotta cheese, parsley, dill, olive oil, egg, salt, and pepper.
2. Mix well.

To assemble the tiropita:

1. Preheat the oven to 375 degrees F (190 degrees C).
2. Grease a 9x13 inch baking dish.
3. Unroll the phyllo dough and cut it into 12 equal pieces.
4. Brush each piece of phyllo dough with melted butter.
5. Layer 6 pieces of phyllo dough in the bottom of the prepared baking dish.
6. Spread the cheese filling over the phyllo dough.
7. Top with the remaining 6 pieces of phyllo dough, brushing each piece with melted butter.
8. Bake for 30-35 minutes, or until golden brown.
9. Let cool slightly before serving.

Variants:

- Add other vegetables to the filling, such as chopped spinach, mushrooms, or zucchini.
- Use different types of cheese in the filling, such as goat cheese or mozzarella cheese.
- Add a dollop of Greek yogurt or sour cream to the filling.

Tips:

- To make the tiropita ahead of time, assemble it according to the directions and then refrigerate it for up to 24 hours. When you're ready to bake it, bring it to room temperature and then bake it according to the directions.

- If you don't have a 9x13 inch baking dish, you can use a smaller dish and adjust the cooking time accordingly.

Notes:

- Tiropita is a popular Greek dish.
- It is a flavorful and flaky pastry that is perfect for a family meal.
- Tiropita can be served with a side of salad or soup.

7. Gemista

Ingredients:

- 6 large tomatoes
- 6 large bell peppers
- 6 large zucchini
- 1 cup rice
- 1/2 cup chopped onion
- 1/2 cup chopped carrots
- 1/2 cup chopped celery
- 1/4 cup chopped fresh parsley
- 1/4 cup chopped fresh dill
- 1/4 cup olive oil
- 1/2 cup tomato sauce
- 1/2 cup water
- Salt and pepper to taste

Approximate Nutritional Values:

- Calories: 250
- Fat: 15 grams
- Protein: 10 grams
- Carbohydrates: 30 grams

Complete Detailed Preparation:

1. Preheat the oven to 375 degrees F (190 degrees C).
2. Cut the tops off the tomatoes and scoop out the pulp.
3. Cut the tops off the bell peppers and remove the seeds and ribs.
4. Cut the zucchini in half lengthwise and scoop out the seeds.
5. In a large bowl, combine the rice, onion, carrots, celery, parsley, dill, olive oil, tomato sauce, water, salt, and pepper.
6. Stuff the tomatoes, bell peppers, and zucchini with the rice mixture.
7. Place the stuffed vegetables in a baking dish and add 1/2 cup of water to the bottom of the dish.
8. Bake for 45-60 minutes, or until the vegetables are tender and the rice is cooked through.
9. Serve hot.

Variants:

- Add other vegetables to the stuffing, such as chopped mushrooms, spinach, or feta cheese.
- Use different types of rice in the stuffing, such as brown rice or wild rice.
- Add a dollop of Greek yogurt or sour cream to the top of the stuffed vegetables before baking.

Tips:

- To make the gemista ahead of time, stuff the vegetables according to the directions and then refrigerate them for up to 24 hours. When you're ready to bake them, bring them to room temperature and then bake them according to the directions.

- If you don't have a baking dish, you can use a large skillet or Dutch oven.

Notes:

- Gemista is a popular Greek dish.
- It is a flavorful and hearty dish that is perfect for a family meal.
- Gemista can be served with a side of salad or bread.

8. Fasolada

Ingredients:

- 1 pound dried white beans, sorted and rinsed
- 1 onion, chopped
- 2 cloves garlic, minced
- 1/4 cup olive oil
- 1 teaspoon dried oregano
- 1/2 teaspoon salt
- 1/4 teaspoon black pepper
- 6 cups water
- 1 cup chopped fresh parsley

Approximate Nutritional Values:

- Calories: 250
- Fat: 10 grams
- Protein: 15 grams
- Carbohydrates: 40 grams

Complete Detailed Preparation:

1. In a large pot, combine the beans, onion, garlic, olive oil, oregano, salt, pepper, and water.
2. Bring to a boil over medium heat.
3. Reduce heat to low, cover, and simmer for 1 hour, or until the beans are tender.
4. Stir in the parsley and serve.

Variants:

- Add other vegetables to the fasolada, such as chopped carrots, celery, or potatoes.
- Use different types of beans in the fasolada, such as kidney beans or black beans.
- Add a dollop of Greek yogurt or sour cream to the fasolada before serving.

Tips:

- To make the fasolada ahead of time, cook it according to the directions and then refrigerate it for up to 3 days. When you're ready to serve it, reheat it over medium heat.
- If you don't have dried white beans, you can use canned white beans. However, be sure to rinse the canned beans thoroughly before using them.

Notes:

- Fasolada is a popular Greek dish.
- It is a simple and flavorful soup that is perfect for a winter meal.
- Fasolada can be served with a side of bread or salad.

9. Briam

Ingredients:

- 1 pound potatoes, peeled and sliced
- 1 pound zucchini, sliced
- 1 pound eggplant, peeled and sliced
- 1 pound tomatoes, chopped
- 1 onion, chopped
- 2 cloves garlic, minced
- 1/4 cup olive oil
- 1 teaspoon dried oregano
- 1/2 teaspoon salt
- 1/4 teaspoon black pepper
- 1/2 cup water

Approximate Nutritional Values:

- Calories: 250
- Fat: 15 grams
- Protein: 10 grams
- Carbohydrates: 30 grams

Complete Detailed Preparation:

1. Preheat the oven to 375 degrees F (190 degrees C).
2. In a large bowl, combine the potatoes, zucchini, eggplant, tomatoes, onion, garlic, olive oil, oregano, salt, pepper, and water.
3. Toss to coat.
4. Spread the vegetables in a 9x13 inch baking dish.
5. Bake for 45-60 minutes, or until the vegetables are tender and browned.
6. Serve hot.

Variants:

- Add other vegetables to the briam, such as chopped carrots, celery, or green beans.
- Use different types of vegetables in the briam, such as sweet potatoes, squash, or mushrooms.
- Add a dollop of Greek yogurt or sour cream to the briam before serving.

Tips:

- To make the briam ahead of time, prepare it according to the directions and then refrigerate it for up to 24 hours. When you're ready to bake it, bring it to room temperature and then bake it according to the directions.
- If you don't have a 9x13 inch baking dish, you can use a smaller dish and adjust the cooking time accordingly.

Notes:

- Briam is a popular Greek dish.
- It is a flavorful and hearty dish that is perfect for a family meal.
- Briam can be served with a side of bread or salad.

10. Papoutsakia

Ingredients:

- 6 large eggplants
- 1 pound ground beef
- 1/2 cup chopped onion
- 1/2 cup chopped green bell pepper
- 1/2 cup chopped red bell pepper
- 1/4 cup chopped fresh parsley
- 1/4 cup chopped fresh dill
- 1/4 cup olive oil
- 1 (28 ounce) can crushed tomatoes
- 1/2 cup tomato sauce
- 1 teaspoon dried oregano
- 1/2 teaspoon salt
- 1/4 teaspoon black pepper
- 1/2 cup grated Parmesan cheese
- 1/4 cup bread crumbs

Approximate Nutritional Values:

- Calories: 350
- Fat: 20 grams
- Protein: 25 grams
- Carbohydrates: 30 grams

Complete Detailed Preparation:

1. Preheat the oven to 375 degrees F (190 degrees C).
2. Cut the eggplants in half lengthwise and scoop out the pulp.
3. In a large skillet, brown the ground beef over medium heat.
4. Add the onion, green bell pepper, and red bell pepper and cook until softened.
5. Stir in the parsley, dill, olive oil, crushed tomatoes, tomato sauce, oregano, salt, and pepper.
6. Bring to a simmer and cook for 30 minutes, or until the sauce has thickened.
7. Stuff the eggplant halves with the meat mixture.
8. Sprinkle the Parmesan cheese and bread crumbs over the eggplant halves.
9. Bake for 30-35 minutes, or until the eggplant is tender and the topping is golden brown.
10. Serve hot.

Variants:

- Use different types of meat in the filling, such as ground lamb or pork.
- Add other vegetables to the filling, such as chopped mushrooms or zucchini.
- Top the papoutsakia with a layer of mashed potatoes instead of Parmesan cheese and bread crumbs.

Tips:

- To make the papoutsakia ahead of time, prepare them according to the directions and then refrigerate them for up to 24 hours. When you're ready to bake them, bring them to room temperature and then bake them according to the directions.

- If you don't have a large skillet, you can brown the ground beef in batches.

Notes:

- Papoutsakia is a popular Greek dish.
- It is a flavorful and hearty dish that is perfect for a family meal.
- Papoutsakia can be served with a side of salad or bread.

11. Dolmadakia

Ingredients:

For the filling:

- 1 cup rice
- 1/2 cup chopped onion
- 1/2 cup chopped carrots
- 1/2 cup chopped celery
- 1/4 cup chopped fresh parsley
- 1/4 cup chopped fresh dill
- 1/4 cup olive oil
- 1/2 cup lemon juice
- 1/2 teaspoon salt
- 1/4 teaspoon black pepper

For the grape leaves:

- 1 pound fresh grape leaves
- 1/2 cup olive oil

Approximate Nutritional Values:

- Calories: 200
- Fat: 15 grams
- Protein: 10 grams
- Carbohydrates: 25 grams

Complete Detailed Preparation:

For the filling:

1. In a large bowl, combine the rice, onion, carrots, celery, parsley, dill, olive oil, lemon juice, salt, and pepper.
2. Mix well.

To prepare the grape leaves:

1. Remove any stems from the grape leaves.
2. Place the grape leaves in a large bowl and cover them with hot water.
3. Let the grape leaves soak for 15 minutes, or until they are softened.
4. Drain the grape leaves and pat them dry.

To assemble the dolmadakia:

1. Place a grape leaf on a flat surface.
2. Put a spoonful of the filling in the center of the grape leaf.
3. Fold the grape leaf over the filling, starting with the bottom and then the sides.
4. Roll up the grape leaf tightly.
5. Repeat with the remaining grape leaves and filling.

To cook the dolmadakia:

1. In a large pot, combine the dolmadakia with 1 cup of water.
2. Bring to a boil over medium heat.
3. Reduce heat to low, cover, and simmer for 30 minutes, or until the rice is cooked through.

4. Serve hot or cold.

Variants:

- Add other vegetables to the filling, such as chopped mushrooms or zucchini.
- Use different types of leaves to make the dolmadakia, such as cabbage leaves or fig leaves.
- Serve the dolmadakia with a side of yogurt sauce or lemon wedges.

Tips:

- To make the dolmadakia ahead of time, prepare them according to the directions and then refrigerate them for up to 2 days. When you're ready to serve them, bring them to room temperature and then heat them through in a saucepan over medium heat.
- If you don't have fresh grape leaves, you can use canned grape leaves. However, be sure to rinse the canned grape leaves thoroughly before using them.

Notes:

- Dolmadakia is a popular Greek dish.
- It is a flavorful and delicate dish that is perfect for a summer meal.
- Dolmadakia can be served as an appetizer or main course.

12. Stifado

Ingredients:

- 1 pound beef chuck roast, cut into 1-inch cubes
- 1/2 cup flour
- 1/4 cup olive oil
- 1 onion, chopped
- 2 cloves garlic, minced
- 1 cup red wine
- 1 (28 ounce) can crushed tomatoes
- 1/2 cup tomato sauce
- 1 teaspoon dried oregano
- 1/2 teaspoon salt
- 1/4 teaspoon black pepper
- 1 pound small onions, peeled
- 1 pound carrots, peeled and cut into chunks

Approximate Nutritional Values:

- Calories: 400
- Fat: 25 grams
- Protein: 30 grams
- Carbohydrates: 35 grams

Complete Detailed Preparation:

1. Preheat the oven to 325 degrees F (165 degrees C).
2. In a large bowl, combine the beef cubes, flour, olive oil, onion, garlic, red wine, crushed tomatoes, tomato sauce, oregano, salt, and pepper.
3. Mix well to coat the beef.
4. Transfer the beef mixture to a Dutch oven or large pot.
5. Add the small onions and carrots.
6. Bring to a boil over medium heat.
7. Reduce heat to low, cover, and simmer for 2 hours, or until the beef is tender.
8. Serve hot.

Variants:

- Use different types of meat in the stifado, such as lamb or pork.
- Add other vegetables to the stifado, such as chopped potatoes or green beans.
- Serve the stifado with a side of rice or bread.

Tips:

- To make the stifado ahead of time, prepare it according to the directions and then refrigerate it for up to 3 days. When you're ready to serve it, reheat it over medium heat.
- If you don't have a Dutch oven or large pot, you can use a large skillet.

Notes:

- Stifado is a popular Greek dish.
- It is a flavorful and hearty dish that is perfect for a winter meal.

- Stifado can be served with a side of salad or bread.

13. Kleftiko

Ingredients:

- 1 leg of lamb, bone-in (about 7 pounds)
- 1/2 cup olive oil
- 1 tablespoon dried oregano
- 1 tablespoon dried thyme
- 1 teaspoon salt
- 1/2 teaspoon black pepper
- 1 lemon, cut into wedges
- 1 head of garlic, cloves separated and peeled
- 1 cup dry white wine
- 1 cup chicken broth

Approximate Nutritional Values:

- Calories: 500
- Fat: 30 grams
- Protein: 40 grams
- Carbohydrates: 20 grams

Complete Detailed Preparation:

1. Preheat the oven to 325 degrees F (165 degrees C).
2. In a large bowl, combine the lamb, olive oil, oregano, thyme, salt, and pepper.
3. Mix well to coat the lamb.
4. Place the lamb in a roasting pan.
5. Add the lemon wedges, garlic cloves, white wine, and chicken broth to the roasting pan.
6. Cover the roasting pan with aluminum foil.
7. Roast the lamb for 4-5 hours, or until the lamb is tender and falls off the bone.
8. Serve hot.

Variants:

- Use different types of meat in the kleftiko, such as pork or beef.
- Add other vegetables to the kleftiko, such as chopped potatoes or carrots.
- Serve the kleftiko with a side of rice or bread.

Tips:

- To make the kleftiko ahead of time, prepare it according to the directions and then refrigerate it for up to 24 hours. When you're ready to cook it, bring it to room temperature and then roast it according to the directions.
- If you don't have a roasting pan, you can use a large Dutch oven.

Notes:

- Kleftiko is a popular Greek dish.
- It is a flavorful and tender dish that is perfect for a special occasion.
- Kleftiko can be served with a side of salad or bread.

14. Kokoretsi

Ingredients:

- 1 lamb intestine, cleaned
- 1 lamb liver, chopped
- 1 lamb heart, chopped
- 1 lamb lung, chopped
- 1/2 cup chopped onion
- 1/2 cup chopped parsley
- 1/4 cup chopped fresh mint
- 1/4 cup olive oil
- 1 tablespoon lemon juice
- 1 teaspoon salt
- 1/2 teaspoon black pepper
- 1 cup chicken broth

Approximate Nutritional Values:

- Calories: 450
- Fat: 35 grams
- Protein: 30 grams
- Carbohydrates: 25 grams

Complete Detailed Preparation:

1. In a large bowl, combine the lamb intestine, liver, heart, lung, onion, parsley, mint, olive oil, lemon juice, salt, and pepper.
2. Mix well to coat the organs.
3. Thread the organs onto the lamb intestine.
4. Place the kokoretsi in a roasting pan.
5. Add the chicken broth to the roasting pan.
6. Cover the roasting pan with aluminum foil.
7. Roast the kokoretsi for 2-3 hours, or until the organs are cooked through.
8. Serve hot.

Variants:

- Add other organs to the kokoretsi, such as kidneys or spleen.
- Use different types of meat in the kokoretsi, such as pork or beef.
- Serve the kokoretsi with a side of rice or bread.

Tips:

- To make the kokoretsi ahead of time, prepare it according to the directions and then refrigerate it for up to 24 hours. When you're ready to cook it, bring it to room temperature and then roast it according to the directions.
- If you don't have a roasting pan, you can use a large Dutch oven.

Notes:

- Kokoretsi is a popular Greek dish.
- It is a flavorful and hearty dish that is perfect for a special occasion.

- Kokoretsi can be served with a side of salad or bread.

15. Loukaniko

Ingredients:

- 1 pound pork shoulder, ground
- 1 pound pork belly, ground
- 1/2 cup red wine
- 1/4 cup brandy
- 1 tablespoon dried oregano
- 1 tablespoon dried thyme
- 1 teaspoon salt
- 1/2 teaspoon black pepper
- 1 hog casing

Approximate Nutritional Values:

- Calories: 400
- Fat: 30 grams
- Protein: 30 grams
- Carbohydrates: 10 grams

Complete Detailed Preparation:

1. In a large bowl, combine the pork shoulder, pork belly, red wine, brandy, oregano, thyme, salt, and pepper.
2. Mix well to combine.
3. Stuff the pork mixture into the hog casing.
4. Tie the ends of the casing securely.
5. Smoke the loukaniko over low heat for 4-6 hours, or until the internal temperature reaches 160 degrees F (71 degrees C).
6. Let the loukaniko cool completely before slicing and serving.

Variants:

- Add other spices to the loukaniko, such as paprika, cumin, or coriander.
- Use different types of meat in the loukaniko, such as lamb or beef.
- Serve the loukaniko with a side of rice or bread.

Tips:

- To make the loukaniko ahead of time, prepare it according to the directions and then refrigerate it for up to 2 weeks. When you're ready to cook it, bring it to room temperature and then smoke it according to the directions.
- If you don't have a smoker, you can cook the loukaniko in a preheated oven at 325 degrees F (165 degrees C) for 1-2 hours, or until the internal temperature reaches 160 degrees F (71 degrees C).

Notes:

- Loukaniko is a popular Greek sausage.
- It is a flavorful and versatile sausage that can be used in a variety of dishes.
- Loukaniko can be served as an appetizer, main course, or side dish.

16. Xoriatiki Salata

Ingredients:

- 1 cucumber, chopped
- 1 tomato, chopped
- 1 green bell pepper, chopped
- 1 red bell pepper, chopped
- 1 onion, chopped
- 1/2 cup feta cheese, crumbled
- 1/4 cup Kalamata olives, pitted and chopped
- 1/4 cup red wine vinegar
- 1/4 cup olive oil
- 1 teaspoon dried oregano
- 1/2 teaspoon salt
- 1/4 teaspoon black pepper

Approximate Nutritional Values:

- Calories: 200
- Fat: 15 grams
- Protein: 10 grams
- Carbohydrates: 25 grams

Complete Detailed Preparation:

1. In a large bowl, combine the cucumber, tomato, green bell pepper, red bell pepper, onion, feta cheese, olives, red wine vinegar, olive oil, oregano, salt, and pepper.
2. Mix well to combine.
3. Serve immediately or refrigerate for later.

Variants:

- Add other vegetables to the xoriatiki salata, such as chopped zucchini or carrots.
- Use different types of cheese in the xoriatiki salata, such as goat cheese or mozzarella cheese.
- Add a dollop of Greek yogurt or sour cream to the xoriatiki salata before serving.

Tips:

- To make the xoriatiki salata ahead of time, prepare it according to the directions and then refrigerate it for up to 24 hours. When you're ready to serve it, bring it to room temperature and then toss it gently.
- If you don't have red wine vinegar, you can use white wine vinegar or lemon juice instead.

Notes:

- Xoriatiki salata is a popular Greek salad.
- It is a refreshing and flavorful salad that is perfect for a summer meal.
- Xoriatiki salata can be served as an appetizer or side dish.

17. Tzatziki

Ingredients:

- 1 cucumber, peeled and grated
- 1 cup plain Greek yogurt
- 1/2 cup olive oil
- 1 tablespoon lemon juice
- 1 clove garlic, minced
- 1/4 cup chopped fresh dill
- 1/4 cup chopped fresh parsley
- Salt and pepper to taste

Approximate Nutritional Values:

- Calories: 150
- Fat: 10 grams
- Protein: 10 grams
- Carbohydrates: 15 grams

Complete Detailed Preparation:

1. In a large bowl, combine the cucumber, Greek yogurt, olive oil, lemon juice, garlic, dill, parsley, salt, and pepper.
2. Mix well to combine.
3. Cover the bowl and refrigerate for at least 2 hours, or overnight.

Variants:

- Add other vegetables to the tzatziki, such as chopped tomatoes or onions.
- Use different types of herbs in the tzatziki, such as mint or oregano.
- Add a dollop of sour cream or mayonnaise to the tzatziki for a richer flavor.

Tips:

- To make the tzatziki ahead of time, prepare it according to the directions and then refrigerate it for up to 3 days. When you're ready to serve it, bring it to room temperature and then stir it well.
- If you don't have a grater, you can chop the cucumber finely with a knife.

Notes:

- Tzatziki is a popular Greek sauce.
- It is a refreshing and flavorful sauce that is perfect for dipping vegetables, meat, or bread.
- Tzatziki can be served as an appetizer, side dish, or condiment.

18. Taramosalata

Ingredients:

- 1 pound cod roe, soaked in water for 2 hours
- 1 cup bread crumbs
- 1/2 cup olive oil
- 1/4 cup lemon juice
- 1/4 cup chopped onion
- 1/4 cup chopped parsley
- 1/4 teaspoon salt
- 1/4 teaspoon black pepper

Approximate Nutritional Values:

- Calories: 200
- Fat: 15 grams
- Protein: 10 grams
- Carbohydrates: 25 grams

Complete Detailed Preparation:

1. Drain the cod roe and remove any membranes.
2. In a food processor, combine the cod roe, bread crumbs, olive oil, lemon juice, onion, parsley, salt, and pepper.
3. Process until smooth.
4. Transfer the taramosalata to a serving bowl and refrigerate for at least 2 hours, or overnight.

Variants:

- Add other ingredients to the taramosalata, such as chopped capers or olives.
- Use different types of bread crumbs in the taramosalata, such as panko or matzo meal.
- Add a dollop of Greek yogurt or sour cream to the taramosalata for a lighter flavor.

Tips:

- To make the taramosalata ahead of time, prepare it according to the directions and then refrigerate it for up to 3 days. When you're ready to serve it, bring it to room temperature and then stir it well.
- If you don't have a food processor, you can mash the cod roe and bread crumbs together with a fork.

Notes:

- Taramosalata is a popular Greek dip.
- It is a flavorful and creamy dip that is perfect for dipping vegetables, crackers, or bread.
- Taramosalata can be served as an appetizer, side dish, or condiment.

19. Htipiti

Ingredients:

- 1 pound feta cheese, crumbled
- 1 cup roasted red peppers, chopped
- 1/2 cup olive oil
- 1/4 cup lemon juice
- 1/4 cup chopped onion
- 1/4 cup chopped parsley
- 1/4 teaspoon salt
- 1/4 teaspoon black pepper

Approximate Nutritional Values:

- Calories: 250
- Fat: 20 grams
- Protein: 15 grams
- Carbohydrates: 10 grams

Complete Detailed Preparation:

1. In a food processor, combine the feta cheese, roasted red peppers, olive oil, lemon juice, onion, parsley, salt, and pepper.
2. Process until smooth.
3. Transfer the htipiti to a serving bowl and refrigerate for at least 2 hours, or overnight.

Variants:

- Add other ingredients to the htipiti, such as chopped olives or capers.
- Use different types of cheese in the htipiti, such as goat cheese or mozzarella cheese.
- Add a dollop of Greek yogurt or sour cream to the htipiti for a lighter flavor.

Tips:

- To make the htipiti ahead of time, prepare it according to the directions and then refrigerate it for up to 3 days. When you're ready to serve it, bring it to room temperature and then stir it well.
- If you don't have a food processor, you can mash the feta cheese and roasted red peppers together with a fork.

Notes:

- Htipiti is a popular Greek dip.
- It is a flavorful and creamy dip that is perfect for dipping vegetables, crackers, or bread.
- Htipiti can be served as an appetizer, side dish, or condiment.

20. Skordalia

Ingredients:

- 1 pound potatoes, peeled and boiled
- 1/2 cup olive oil
- 1/4 cup lemon juice
- 1/4 cup chopped garlic
- 1/4 cup chopped parsley
- 1/4 teaspoon salt
- 1/4 teaspoon black pepper

Approximate Nutritional Values:

- Calories: 200
- Fat: 15 grams
- Protein: 10 grams
- Carbohydrates: 25 grams

Complete Detailed Preparation:

1. In a food processor, combine the potatoes, olive oil, lemon juice, garlic, parsley, salt, and pepper.
2. Process until smooth.
3. Transfer the skordalia to a serving bowl and refrigerate for at least 2 hours, or overnight.

Variants:

- Add other ingredients to the skordalia, such as chopped walnuts or almonds.
- Use different types of potatoes in the skordalia, such as sweet potatoes or russet potatoes.
- Add a dollop of Greek yogurt or sour cream to the skordalia for a lighter flavor.

Tips:

- To make the skordalia ahead of time, prepare it according to the directions and then refrigerate it for up to 3 days. When you're ready to serve it, bring it to room temperature and then stir it well.
- If you don't have a food processor, you can mash the potatoes and garlic together with a fork.

Notes:

- Skordalia is a popular Greek dip.
- It is a flavorful and creamy dip that is perfect for dipping vegetables, crackers, or bread.
- Skordalia can be served as an appetizer, side dish, or condiment.

Conclusion

As we reach the end of our culinary journey through the vibrant and diverse cuisine of the Jews of Greece, we can't help but marvel at the rich tapestry of flavors and traditions that have been woven together over centuries.

From the humble beginnings of Sephardic immigrants who brought their culinary heritage from Spain and Portugal, to the modern-day fusion of Greek and Jewish influences, the cuisine of the Jews of Greece has evolved into a unique and captivating blend.

We have explored the intricacies of traditional dishes such as spanakopita, pastitsio, and avgolemono soup, while also delving into the more modern creations that have emerged from the vibrant Jewish communities of Athens, Thessaloniki, and beyond.

Through recipes passed down through generations and the unwavering dedication of Jewish cooks and chefs, the culinary traditions of the Jews of Greece have not only survived but have flourished. They have become an integral part of the country's cultural fabric and a testament to the resilience and creativity of the Jewish people.

As we close the pages of this cookbook, we invite you to continue exploring the culinary delights of the Jews of Greece. Experiment with new recipes, gather with friends and family to share traditional dishes, and savor the rich flavors that have shaped this unique and unforgettable cuisine.

And as you do, remember the wry observation of the great Greek philosopher, Epicurus: "The greatest wealth is to live content with little." May the culinary traditions of the Jews of Greece continue to bring joy and fulfillment to your table for generations to come.

Made in the USA
Monee, IL
12 September 2024